Published by Creative Education
P.O. Box 227, Mankato, Minnesota 56002
Creative Education is an imprint of The Creative Company

Design and production by Blue Design
Printed in the United States of America

Photographs by Getty Images (Diamond Images, Focus on Sport, FPG, Stephen Green/MLB Photos, MLB Photos, National Baseball Hall of Fame Library/MLB Photos, Photo File/MLB Photos, Pictorial Parade, Tom Pidgeon, Rich Pilling/MLB Photos, TONY RANZE/AFP, Mark Rucker/Transcendental Graphics, Frank Schershel/Time & Life Pictures, Gregory Shamus, Tony Tomsic/MLB Photos, Ron Vesely/MLB Photos), Bryan Hunter

Library of Congress Cataloging-in-Publication Data

Gilbert, Sara.
The story of the Detroit Tigers / by Sara Gilbert.
p. cm. — (Baseball: the great American game)
Includes index.
ISBN-13: 978-1-58341-487-3
1. Detroit Tigers (Baseball team)—History—Juvenile literature. I. Title. II. Series.

GV875.D6G55 2007
796.357'640977434—dc22   2006027467

First Edition
9 8 7 6 5 4 3 2 1

Cover: Outfielder Ty Cobb
Page 1: Outfielder Sam Crawford
Page 3: Pitcher Justin Verlander

THE STORY OF THE
DETROIT TIGERS

by Sara Gilbert

KIRK GIBSON

Detroit Tigers

The Detroit Tigers are clinging to a one-run lead as right fielder Kirk Gibson steps to the plate to face San Diego Padres pitcher Goose Gossage in the bottom of the eighth inning. Gibson glances toward the dugout to see his manager, Sparky Anderson, flashing him four fingers—a sign that he should expect to be walked. But Gibson flashes back a sign of his own: 10 fingers, initiating a $10 bet that Gossage will pitch to him instead. And despite being asked by his manager to throw balls, Gossage does. He comes at Gibson, who had hit 27 home runs during the regular season and one earlier in the game, with a slider that rides high across the plate. Gibson slams it into the outfield seats, then takes a victory lap around the bases, punching the air all the way. Three outs later, his Tigers win the 1984 World Series, bringing a fourth world championship home to Detroit.

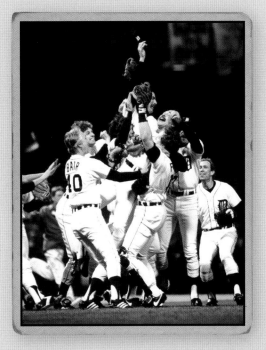

ON THE PROWL

ince the early 1900s, Detroit, Michigan, has been known as the "Motor City," a nickname earned when Henry Ford built his first car there in 1896 and later invented the assembly line form of production, which made motor vehicles widely available to the public. Ford's plant was followed by many others, making Detroit the car capital of the world.

By the time those cars were rolling off the factory floor, Detroit had something else to call its own: the Detroit Tigers, a major league baseball team that joined the American League (AL) when it was formed in 1901. The Tigers earned their nickname because of their black and yellow striped socks, but quickly lived up to the animal's reputation for ferocity as well. In their first game on April 25, 1901, the Tigers rallied from a seemingly insurmountable 13–4 deficit in the ninth inning to win 14–13.

Such remarkable wins became expected in Detroit, especially after the team added a fearless 18-year-old outfielder named Ty Cobb to the roster in 1905. Cobb spent the next two decades setting and breaking records—many of which still stand today. In 1907, his .350 batting average was the best in the league and earned "The Georgia Peach" the first of nine straight AL batting

TY COBB – Cobb's approach to the game was summed up by his high and hard slides, and this after he sometimes sharpened his spikes with a file in view of opposing fielders before games. He remained a villain to many even as he became a legend of the game.

TIGERS AT "THE CORNER"

When the Tigers took the field on April 25, 1901, they played in Bennett Park, a small, often crowded stadium situated at the corner of Michigan Avenue and Trumbull Street in Detroit. For almost a full century, the team continued to play at "The Corner" in different incarnations of their original stadium. The first change came in 1912, when owner Frank Navin invested $300,000 to build a much larger concrete and steel stadium on the same corner. The new park could hold 23,000 fans—almost five times more than Bennett Park. Over the next quarter century, the stadium, which was named Briggs Stadium in 1938 after new owner Walter Briggs, was modified often, including the addition of lights in 1948. In 1961, with seating now available for 53,000 fans, it was renamed Tiger Stadium, a moniker that stuck for the next 32 years. But on September 27, 1999, the team played its last game on the hallowed corner of Michigan and Trumbull. The Tigers abandoned "The Corner" for Comerica Park, a $300-million stadium in downtown Detroit designed to combine the classic feel of Tiger Stadium with the amenities expected at modern ballparks.

titles. Cobb's boastful, aggressive personality didn't win him a lot of friends, but no one could deny his ability. "Ty Cobb is a low-down, miserable excuse for a human being," said Tigers right fielder Sam Crawford. "He's also the best player I've ever seen."

Cobb and Crawford were just two of the many talented players who led the Tigers to three AL pennants from 1907 to 1909. But as much as they dominated the regular season, the Tigers struggled against more experienced opponents from the National League (NL) in the postseason. They fell to the Chicago Cubs twice in the World Series, and in 1909, the Pittsburgh Pirates topped Detroit 8–0 in the deciding Game 7.

SAM CRAWFORD

In 1901, speedster Sam Crawford set a major-league record by hitting 12 inside-the-park home runs.

The Tigers lost their swagger after that trio of disappointments. Suddenly, they could finish no higher than second in the AL. Then, when the team christened its new home, Navin Field, in 1912, it struggled to a sixth-place finish with a 69–84 record. Although the 1915 season ended with the Tigers just two and a half games shy of the AL pennant, Detroit remained mired in the middle of the pack for the next several years.

Cobb's constant pursuit of batting titles was challenged briefly by Tigers right fielder Harry Heilmann, whose .394 average in 1921 was the best in the league. Two years later, Heilmann topped .400—making him the only Tigers player beside Cobb to do so. But even with such strong swingers in the lineup, Detroit spent most of the 1920s stranded near the bottom of the standings.

NAVIN FIELD

NAVIN FIELD – Renamed Briggs Stadium in 1938 and then Tiger Stadium in 1961, Navin Field was eventually home to both the Tigers and pro football's Detroit Lions. It opened in 1912 on the same day that the Boston Red Sox christened Fenway Park.

Although his fielding ability was average, Harry Heilmann's marvelous hitting put him in the Hall of Fame.

PITCHER · JACK MORRIS

Although Jack Morris never won the Cy Young Award, he was one of the most reliable pitchers of his time. In his 18-year career, he tallied 10 or more wins in 14 seasons—and 3 times totaled 20 or more. He started the Tigers' 1984 world championship campaign off right by hurling a no-hitter on April 7, the first of his 19 wins that season. Morris's fiery pitches were matched by his fierce nature; he often found himself in feuds with reporters or spats with teammates. Still, his strong arm was missed when he left the Tigers to play for the Minnesota Twins in 1991.

JACK MORRIS
PITCHER

DETROIT TIGERS

STATS

Tigers seasons: 1977–90

Height: 6-3

Weight: 200

- **5-time All-Star**

- **254 career wins**

- **2,478 career strikeouts**

- ***The Sporting News*' 1981 AL Pitcher of the Year**

CHARLIE GEHRINGER

BREAKING THE CENTURY MARK

Although the 1934 season ended in heartbreak for the Detroit Tigers, it still ranks as the team's best overall effort. Led by first-year manager and catcher Mickey Cochrane, the Tigers won 21 of their games in April and May. It was in June, however, that the team really began to pick up steam, winning 19 and losing just 8. On June 15, young right-handed pitcher Lynwood "Schoolboy" Rowe earned an 11–4 victory against the Boston Red Sox and proceeded to win his next 15 starts to compile a 16-game winning streak, tying Washington Senators pitcher Walter Johnson's 1912 record. Rowe's streak was complemented by the Tigers' 14-game winning

streak in July and August. Along the way, second baseman Charlie Gehringer also compiled the most hits (214) and runs scored (134) in the league. By the time the season ended on the last day of September, Cochrane's Tigers had amassed 101 wins, the most in team history until 1968, when the squad recorded 103. But both the 1968 season and the 104-win season in 1984 were played on the extended schedule of 162 games, as opposed to the 154 games played in 1934. Therefore, the 1934 Tigers' winning percentage of .656 remains a team record.

REGAINING THE ROAR

Twenty-five years after their last AL championship in 1909, the Detroit Tigers finally found themselves atop the standings again in 1934—and they did it without Babe Ruth, whom team owner Frank Navin had desperately wanted to acquire. Instead, he paid $100,000 for Mickey Cochrane, who joined the team in 1934 as both catcher and manager. With slugger Hank Greenberg at first and the almost-flawless Charlie Gehringer at second, Cochrane led the team to a 101–53 finish, seven games ahead of the New York Yankees. But again, the Tigers were outplayed in the World Series, falling to the St. Louis Cardinals after a crushing 11–0 loss in Game 7.

That was all the disappointment the team could take. Detroit came back with a vengeance in 1935. Greenberg's AL Most Valuable Player (MVP) season, in which he clobbered 36 home runs, propelled the team back to the "Fall Classic," where Detroit faced the Cubs. Although the Cubs shut them out in Game 1, the Tigers bounced back to win the next three games. The Tigers were determined not to disappoint their fans again—and finally, they didn't. With Game 6 tied 3–3 in the bottom of the ninth, a ringing single by left fielder Leon "Goose" Goslin sent Cochrane hustling home from second base.

CHARLIE GEHRINGER

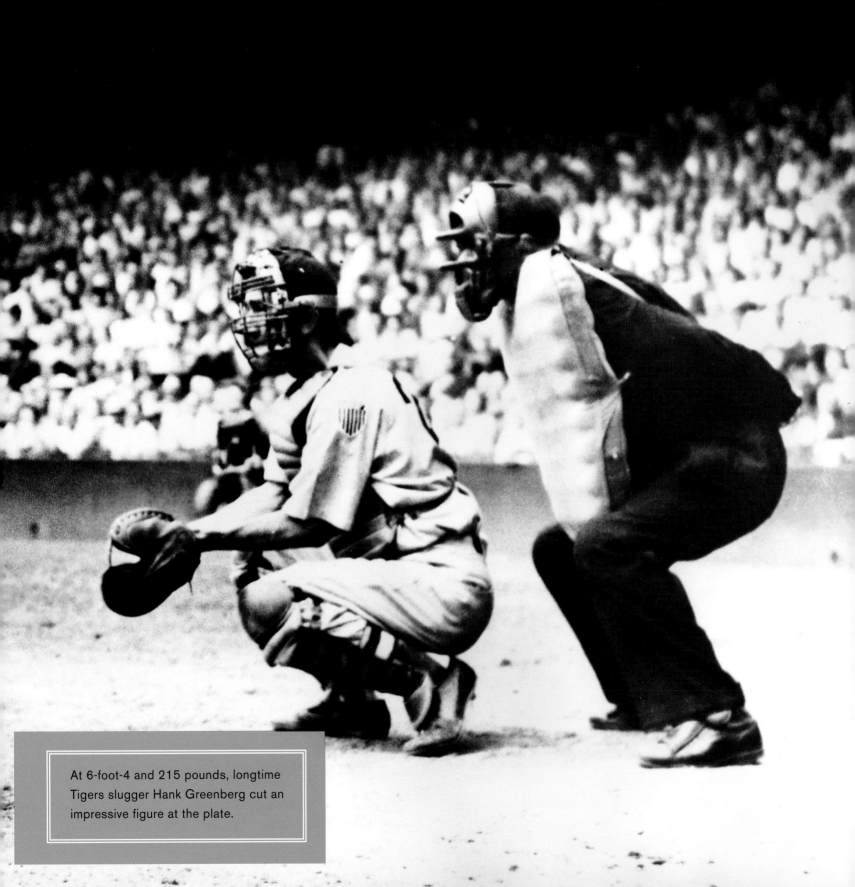

At 6-foot-4 and 215 pounds, longtime Tigers slugger Hank Greenberg cut an impressive figure at the plate.

FIFTH TIME'S A CHARM

By the time the Detroit Tigers won the AL pennant in 1935, the team had already played in four World Series—and had lost all of them. Two of those had been against the Chicago Cubs, whom the Tigers were set to face again in 1935. Again, the Cubs took an early series lead with a 3–0 shutout in Game 1. But the Tigers refused to be intimidated. Instead, they came back to win the second game 8–3, courtesy of a home run by AL MVP Hank Greenberg, and to steal Game 3 in an 11-inning affair that ended 6–5. When Detroit won again in Game 4, it looked like the Tigers might finally take home the trophy. But then Chicago won Game 5, prolonging the series for at least one more game. That game was in Detroit, on October 7, 1935. In the bottom of the ninth, the score was knotted up 3–3. Then Mickey Cochrane singled and advanced to second on a fielder's choice. As Goose Goslin came to the plate, Cochrane led off toward third. And when Goslin slammed a single into the outfield, Cochrane raced home. In their fifth try, the Tigers had finally won the trophy.

The Tigers had finally become world champions, and the jubilant hometown fans celebrated the long overdue title.

The fans' delight in Detroit's success was short-lived, though. The Tigers finished a distant second in the AL the next two years and slipped further in the standings as the '30s came to a close. But that changed in 1940, when another MVP campaign by Greenberg and a 21-win season by pitcher Bobo Newsom helped Detroit win the pennant by a single game. Then, with the World Series against the Cincinnati Reds tied up at three games apiece, manager Del Baker asked Newsom to take the mound after only a day's rest. "He called upon his mighty Bobo Newsom, and Bobo, already the dramatic hero of the series, answered the challenge with equal courage," *The New York Times* reported. But the task was too much even for Newsom; the Tigers lost the game, 2–1, and the series.

As the next season started, so did the United States' involvement in World War II. The Tigers weren't the only team to lose players to the war, but they were hit hard. Greenberg was one of the first players to enlist, leaving Detroit early in 1941. Without their heavy hitter, the Tigers struggled—until a new MVP entered the picture in 1944. Southpaw hurler Hal Newhouser notched 29 wins in his award-winning season, closely followed by pitcher Dizzy Trout, who had 27. Although their success kept the team in the race, the Tigers missed the AL pennant by one excruciating game.

CATCHER · BILL FREEHAN

In 1964, Bill Freehan represented the Tigers in the All-Star Game and continued to do so for the next 10 years, including 7 as a starter. Freehan, a Detroit boy, was most respected for his defensive skills; when he retired, he held major-league records for chances (10,734) and putouts (9,941) and boasted the highest fielding average for a catcher until 2002.

Freehan's bat also matured as he aged. He hit 25 home runs with 84 RBI in 1968, helping lead the Tigers to the World Series. He helped the team win the series too, recording the final out in Game 7 by catching a lazy pop foul.

BILL FREEHAN
CATCHER

DETROIT
TIGERS

STATS

Tigers seasons: 1961, 1963–76

Height: 6-2

Weight: 205

- **11-time All-Star**

- **5-time Gold Glove winner**

- **200 career HR**

- **758 career RBI**

Newhouser got some much-needed help from the offense in 1945 when Greenberg returned in the second half of the season. The team surged ahead of the Washington Nationals to win the pennant and take its seventh trip to the World Series. With many players still on active duty in the war, no one expected much out of the 1945 series. But with Greenberg back in the lineup and Newhouser on the mound, the Tigers had the advantage over the Cubs yet again. They won the series with a crushing 9–3 victory in Game 7. As the last out was recorded, the joyous Tigers rushed the mound to congratulate Newhouser. The Motor City had its second world championship.

HAL NEWHOUSER

Kept out of World War II by a heart problem, Hal Newhouser led the AL in wins four times in the 1940s.

FIRST BASEMAN · HANK GREENBERG

Hank Greenberg was never the most graceful player on the diamond. But he made up for his awkwardness in the field with his power at the plate. He hit 40 or more home runs in 4 seasons and made a run at Babe Ruth's record of 60 in 1938, when he finished the season with 58. Greenberg was one of the first big-league players to join the army in 1941 and spent four years serving in World War II. Despite that absence from the game, he compiled 331 home runs in his Hall of Fame career and went on to become a general manager and owner of the Cleveland Indians.

HANK GREENBERG
FIRST BASEMAN

DETROIT
TIGERS

STATS

Tigers seasons: 1930, 1933–41, 1945–46

Height: 6-4

Weight: 215

- **2-time AL MVP**

- **5-time All-Star**

- **1,276 career RBI**

- **Baseball Hall of Fame inductee (1956)**

All of America was in a celebratory mood when Detroit won the 1945 World Series, as World War II had ended just two months before.

AL KALINE – Kaline earned the nickname "Mr. Tiger" by spending every one of his 22 big-league seasons in a Detroit uniform. During those years, the classy outfielder set many franchise records, including most games played (2,834) and most home runs (399).

TIGERS

YOUNG CATS

etroit fans would have to wait more than 20 years for another trophy. The Tigers tried valiantly in 1946 and 1947 but finished second both years. After the 1946 attempt, Greenberg moved on to spend his last major-league season with the Pittsburgh Pirates, leaving Detroit without a bona fide offensive threat. But in the midst of the mediocre seasons that followed, a few new stars were born.

The first was George Kell, a third baseman signed by Detroit in 1946. He finished his first year batting .322 and proceeded to hit .300 or better for the next five seasons. Although he was not a power hitter, his consistency at the plate kept the Tigers competitive in the late 1940s and early '50s. Kell helped the team dominate the AL for most of 1950, but Detroit sputtered late and ultimately finished in second place.

A year after enduring their worst season ever in 1952 (when they went 50–104), the Tigers signed a promising young right fielder to pull them out of their slump: 18-year-old Al Kaline. Although a slick fielder, the slender youngster struggled at the plate in his first year. Then Boston Red Sox great Ted Williams told him to strengthen his wrists by squeezing baseballs as hard as he could. That advice paid off; in 1955, at the age of 20 and with a .340 average, Kaline became the youngest player in history to win the AL batting title. "In my book, he's the greatest right-handed batter in the league," Williams said of Kaline. "There's no telling how far the kid could go."

Despite the talents of Kaline, Kell, and third baseman Harvey Kuenn, the Tigers didn't get higher than fourth place for the next few years. Pitcher Frank Lary led the league with 21 wins in 1956, and Kuenn was the league's leader in hits four times in the 1950s, but still the Tigers struggled to stay above .500 and out of the AL cellar.

In 1961, New York Yankees outfielder Roger Maris spent the season chasing (and ultimately surpassing) Babe Ruth's hallowed single-season home run record. At the same time, Tigers first baseman Norm Cash hit 41 home runs with 132 RBI and posted a league-best .361 batting average, helping his team win 101 games. Unfortunately, that still left Detroit eight games behind Maris and the Yankees, out of postseason play again.

Behind solid hitting by Kuenn and Kaline, the Tigers put together winning seasons five of the next six years. Still, they stayed well out of contention until 1967. Then, with right-hander Earl Wilson picking up 22 wins on the mound and four players hitting 20 or more home runs, the Tigers were suddenly involved in one of the tightest pennant races in major-league history, one that came down to the last game of the season. Had the Tigers not lost that game 8–5 to the California Angels, they could have made it to the World Series. Instead, Detroit's loss allowed the Red Sox all the room they needed to nudge past to claim the pennant.

SECOND BASEMAN · CHARLIE GEHRINGER

Charlie Gehringer's nickname, "The Mechanical Man," was a perfect fit for a player who moved like clockwork at second base and was remarkably consistent at the plate. He was also known as a quiet man who lacked the colorful personality of some of his Detroit teammates. Gehringer preferred to let his talent speak for itself. He led the AL in assists and fielding percentage seven times, won the league MVP award in 1937, and hit better than .300 in a season 13 times in his brilliant career. After his playing days, he served as the Tigers' general manager and vice president.

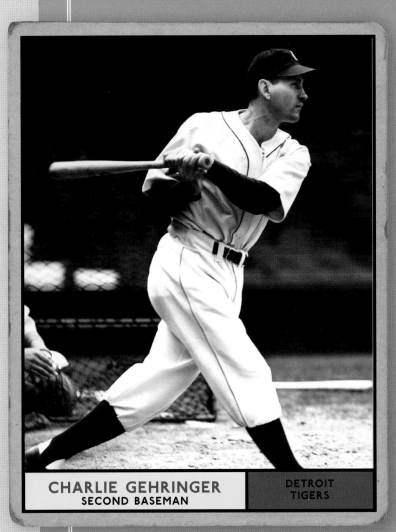

CHARLIE GEHRINGER
SECOND BASEMAN

DETROIT TIGERS

STATS

Tigers seasons: 1924–42

Height: 5-11

Weight: 180

- .320 career BA

- 1937 AL MVP

- 1929 AL leader in stolen bases (27)

- Baseball Hall of Fame inductee (1949)

DENNY McLAIN

TIGERS RISING

S uch late-season heartache would not follow the Tigers into 1968. After losing on opening day, Detroit went on a nine-game winning streak, setting the stage for an incredible 103-win season. Pitcher Denny McLain was the star; when he won his 30th game on September 14, the crowd at Tiger Stadium stood and chanted, "We want Denny! We want Denny!" until he emerged from the dugout for an ovation. McLain wasn't the only hero, though: left fielder Willie Horton led the team with 36 home runs and a .285 average, and the Tigers finished 12 games ahead of the closest AL contender.

Detroit faced the defending champion St. Louis Cardinals in the World Series and quickly fell behind, three games to one. But in Game 5, Detroit pitcher Mickey Lolich held the Cards to three runs, and Kaline put the Tigers ahead for good with a bases-loaded single in the seventh inning. In Game 6, Detroit scored 10 runs in the third inning and ended up winning 13–1. That set up a tense pitcher's duel in Game 7: St. Louis's dominant Bob Gibson against Lolich. The game was scoreless until the seventh inning, when a line drive off the bat of Tigers center fielder Jim Northrup cleared the bases. Detroit refused to relinquish its lead and won the series four games to three. Thousands of Tigers fans

Brash hurler Denny McLain was brilliant in the late 1960s, winning the Cy Young Award in 1968 and 1969.

THIRD BASEMAN · GEORGE KELL

George Kell got his big break by being available to play for the Philadelphia Athletics when World War II pulled many big-league players away from their teams. But long after the war ended, Kell remained in the majors and became one of the best third basemen of his time. He stole the AL batting title from Red Sox great Ted Williams in 1949, finishing with a .343 average—two ten-thousandths of a point better than Williams. That same year, Kell set a record for the fewest strikeouts (13) by a batting champion in major-league history. He remained with the Tigers as their play-by-play announcer after retiring.

GEORGE KELL
THIRD BASEMAN

DETROIT TIGERS

STATS

Tigers seasons: 1946–52

Height: 5-9

Weight: 175

- **10-time All-Star**
- **2,054 career hits**
- **.306 career BA**
- **Baseball Hall of Fame inductee (1983)**

turned out to welcome the world champions home. "The entire downtown was jammed," McLain later recalled. "There were so many people waiting to meet our plane, they had to close the airport. At the time, the world seemed wonderfully warm."

The warmth didn't last long for McLain. In 1970, he was suspended from baseball for placing bets and was later sentenced to prison on gambling and drug charges. The Tigers lost another leader when Kaline retired in 1974, shortly after collecting his 3,000th hit. The team struggled, posting a woeful 57–102 record in 1975.

Just when everyone in Detroit needed something to smile about, the Tigers signed a pitcher named Mark Fidrych. Fidrych, who became better known as "The Bird," amused fans and teammates alike with his antics on the mound. He won 19 games in 1976, earning AL Rookie of the Year honors. But it was the conversations that he had with the ball before delivering each pitch that drew fans to Tiger Stadium and attracted media attention. "He was the game's Pied Piper, the most charismatic player I've ever seen in baseball," said Tigers announcer Ernie Harwell. "Everywhere he went that year, people followed in droves. It was phenomenal."

But for all of Fidrych's sweet-talking, the Tigers were able to muster only

Mark Fidrych's big-league career was colorful but short, as he won 19 games as a rookie but just 10 after that.

MARK FIDRYCH

SHORTSTOP · ALAN TRAMMELL

Alan Trammell started out as an unremarkable shortstop in 1977. But before long, he became one of the best in the league, pairing with second baseman Lou Whitaker to form the most enduring keystone combination in major-league history: in his 20-year career, Trammell helped turn 1,307 double plays. In 1984, league managers voted him the smartest, best defensive infielder in the game. He helped take Detroit to the World Series that year and, after driving in all four Tigers runs in Game 4, was named series MVP. Trammell returned to the Tigers as manager in 2003 and led the team until 2005.

ALAN TRAMMELL
SHORTSTOP

DETROIT
TIGERS

STATS

Tigers seasons: 1977–96 (2003–05 as manager)

Height: 6-0

Weight: 175

- 6-time All-Star

- 4-time Gold Glove winner

- 2,365 career hits

- 1984 World Series MVP

LEFT FIELDER · SAM CRAWFORD

Sam Crawford's specialty was the rarest hit in baseball: the triple. In his 19-year career, he tallied 309 three-baggers, still the most in baseball history, just ahead of teammate Ty Cobb. Crawford, a likeable, easygoing player, disliked Cobb intensely—yet the two of them were in agreement when it came to base running, often pulling off daring double steals. Crawford ended his career just shy of 3,000 hits, with 366 stolen bases and 1,525 RBI. He was elected into the Hall of Fame in 1957, thanks in large part to a campaign led by Cobb.

STATS

Tigers seasons: 1903–17

Height: 6-0

Weight: 190

- **2,961 career hits**
- **3-time AL leader in RBI**
- **.309 career BA**
- **Baseball Hall of Fame inductee (1957)**

SAM CRAWFORD
LEFT FIELDER

DETROIT
TIGERS

LUCKY 11

In 1978, the Tigers ended an abysmal string of four straight losing seasons by finishing with an 86–76 record. The winning change of pace was so refreshing that they kept it going for 11 straight years, not posting another losing record until they ended the 1989 season with a miserable 59–103 mark. During that winning run, the Tigers won a total of 951 regular-season games, including a club-record 104 in 1984. Part of their success could certainly be attributed to the motivation of Hall of Fame manager Sparky Anderson, who had joined the team in 1979 and promised to win a pennant within five years. But part of it could also be credited to fiery pitcher Jack Morris, who won 173 games during that stretch and became baseball's winningest pitcher of the 1980s. Anderson and Morris had a fine supporting cast as well, particularly sluggers Kirk Gibson and Lance Parrish and infielders Alan Trammell and Lou Whitaker. Although the Tigers would qualify for postseason play only twice during those 11 winning years, they did manage to cap one of those seasons, 1984, with their first world championship in almost two decades.

TIGERS

[35]

a 74–87 finish. The next year, Fidrych struggled with injuries, and the Tigers again ended with a losing season. Midway through the 1979 season, the Tigers hired a new manager, Sparky Anderson, who had led the Cincinnati Reds to two world championships. Although Anderson couldn't get his young team above fifth place that year, he was determined to at least move it in the right direction.

RETURN OF THE TIGERS

One of Anderson's first announcements when he took over as the Tigers' manager was that his team would win a pennant within five years—a bold prediction he later admitted he had "pulled out of a bag." But each year, his players progressed toward that goal. Fiery young pitcher Jack Morris began a string of 10 years in which he led the team in wins, including a 20-win season in 1983. Catcher Lance Parrish and right fielder Kirk Gibson began perfecting their home run swings, while slick-fielding shortstop Alan Trammell and durable second baseman Lou Whitaker became one of the best double-play duos in the major leagues.

By 1983, the team had broken away from its place in the middle of the pack to finish 92–70, just six games behind the Baltimore Orioles in the AL Eastern Division (the league had been split into two divisions in 1969). And

SPARKY ANDERSON

KIRK GIBSON

PLAYING WITH A SPARK

The Tigers left little doubt that they were a team of destiny in 1984. With skipper Sparky Anderson leading a crew of players cheered on by the popular cry "Bless You Boys," a phrase coined by local sportscaster Al Ackerman, Detroit made quick work of its opponents, compiling a 35–5 record by the middle of May. Although they had secured the AL East crown by the middle of June, the Tigers continued their winning ways, amassing a franchise-record 104 wins. They quickly added three more to that total by sweeping the

Kansas City Royals in the AL Championship Series (ALCS). Then it was off to San Diego to battle the Padres in the World Series. Despite a win in Game 2, the Padres didn't have much of a chance; Detroit dominated the rest of the series. Jack Morris pitched all nine innings of both the first and fourth games, holding San Diego to a total of four runs. When the Tigers won Game 5, they notched their 111th win of the season and the fourth world title in team history.

TIGERS

[37]

CENTER FIELDER · TY COBB

Ty Cobb was one of the greatest players in the history of baseball. He still holds the highest lifetime batting average, a record that is unlikely to be broken, and is second in career hits. He was a daring base stealer who stole second, third, and home in the same inning six different times in his 24-year career! Despite his extraordinary talent, Cobb was one of the most universally disliked players in the history of the game. Teammates and opponents alike despised him for his hostile temperament and his penchant for hard, spikes-up slides— but ultimately respected him for his undeniable ability.

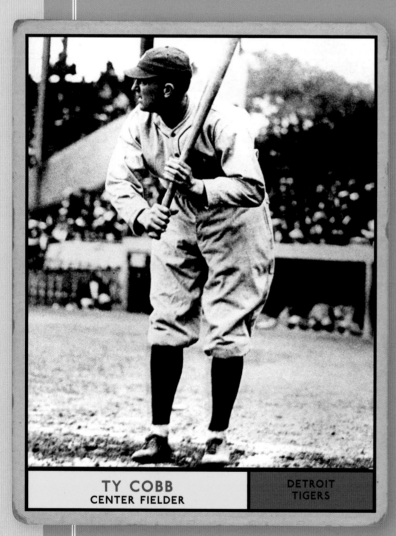

TY COBB
CENTER FIELDER

DETROIT TIGERS

STATS

Tigers seasons: 1905–26

Height: 6-1

Weight: 175

- **.366 career BA**
- **4,189 career hits**
- **6-time AL leader in stolen bases**
- **Baseball Hall of Fame inductee (1936)**

in 1984—exactly five years after Anderson's prediction—the Tigers jumped out to an early lead, buoyed by a Morris no-hitter in the fourth game of the season, and never looked back. By June, the winner of the AL East was apparent; by the time the season ended, Detroit had compiled 104 wins, eclipsing the Toronto Blue Jays by 15 games.

Detroit swept the Kansas City Royals in the ALCS and then moved on to face the San Diego Padres in the World Series. It took only five games, capped off by Gibson's three-run blast in the eighth inning of Game 5, for the Tigers to claim the world championship. As champagne corks popped in the clubhouse after the game, an emotional Anderson climbed atop a stool to address his players. "Don't forget this moment," he said. "You did it all."

The Tigers would not be able to do it again during Anderson's tenure. They came close in 1987, rebounding from an 11–19 start to capture the AL East crown in the last weekend of play, but they lost in the ALCS to the eventual world champion Minnesota Twins. They stayed close in 1988 as well but couldn't repeat their late-season heroics and finished in second place.

After finishing at the bottom of the heap with 103 losses in 1989, the Tigers took a risk on first baseman Cecil Fielder, whose promising career had gone sour in Toronto. It seemed to sweeten in Detroit, though. Fielder hit 51 home runs in 1990 and slammed 44 more with 133 runs batted in (RBI) as the Tigers finished second in the division in 1991. But the entire team's

RIGHT FIELDER · KIRK GIBSON

In the first game of his rookie season, Kirk Gibson hit both a home run and a triple, setting the stage for what turned into an incredible 17-year career in the big leagues. Although he was never an All-Star or a Gold Glove winner, the scruffy outfielder's tenacity made him a favorite with Detroit fans. Gibson had a knack for hitting clutch home runs, including a three-run blast off San Diego Padres pitcher Goose Gossage that sealed a World Series win for the Tigers in 1984. Although Gibson was released by the Tigers in 1987, he returned to Detroit six years later to finish his career.

STATS

Tigers seasons: 1979–87, 1993–95

Height: 6-3

Weight: 215

· **1984 ALCS MVP**

· **870 career RBI**

· **1,553 career hits**

· **260 career doubles**

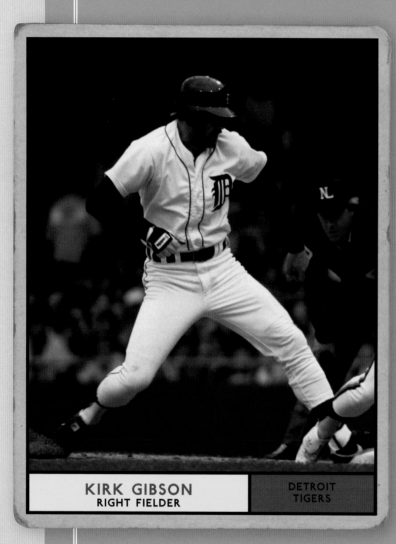

KIRK GIBSON
RIGHT FIELDER

DETROIT TIGERS

production started to slide the next year, and Detroit dropped to sixth place with a disappointing 75–87 record. Although the Tigers bounced back to a winning season in 1993, they remained far out of the playoff picture.

That winning 1993 record marked the last successful season of Sparky Anderson's illustrious career. When the 1995 season ended with his Tigers in fourth place, Anderson announced his retirement. He was voted into the Baseball Hall of Fame five years later, in his first year of eligibility.

TEMPERED TIGERS

nderson's departure was just one of several in the mid-1990s. Gibson and Whitaker both retired in 1995, and Trammell left in 1996. With a reshaped roster that included hard-hitting right fielder Bobby Higginson and slugging first baseman Tony Clark, new manager Buddy Bell saw his tenure begin with a new team record for most losses in a season, as the 1996 Tigers finished 53–109. The slump would continue.

In 1999, the Tigers finished their final season of play in 87-year-old Tiger Stadium before a sold-out crowd of 43,356 fans. The next spring, they opened the 2000 season with every seat filled at their new home, the cavernous Co-

IVAN RODRIGUEZ

Famous for his ability to gun down base stealers, veteran catcher Ivan Rodriguez joined Detroit in 2004.

merica Park. Despite making a competitive showing early in the season, the Tigers faded to finish 79–83.

After two more poor seasons, the Tigers hired longtime fan favorite Alan Trammell as manager, but he could not bring back the magic of seasons past in 2003. Instead, the Tigers lost more games than ever before, posting a 43–119 record that stands as the worst in the history of the AL. "We lost a lot of games, but we can't say it was a complete failure," said optimistic rookie pitcher Jeremy Bonderman, who suffered 19 losses. "A lot of young guys, including myself,

MANAGER · SPARKY ANDERSON

George "Sparky" Anderson played a single season in the majors: in 1959, as a second baseman for the Philadelphia Phillies. But he became better known for his almost 30 years as a manager, both for the Cincinnati Reds and the Detroit Tigers. The charming, jovial Anderson led the Tigers to a World Series championship in 1984, won AL Manager of the Year Awards in 1984 and 1987, and finished his career in 1995 with the third-most managerial wins in major-league history. Along the way, he earned the nickname "Captain Hook" for his tendency to take pitchers out of a game early and send in relievers.

STATS

Tigers seasons as manager: 1979–95

Height: 5-9

Weight: 170

Managerial Record: 2,194–1,834

World Series Championship: 1984

SPARKY ANDERSON
MANAGER

DETROIT
TIGERS

Tigers outfielders Magglio Ordóñez (left), Curtis Granderson (middle), and Alexis Gomez in 2006.

THE FORGETTABLE SEASON

There was good cause for optimism in Detroit at the start of the 2003 season. Alan Trammell, the team's longtime shortshop, had come back to manage the Tigers—and had brought along two of his World Series-winning teammates, Kirk Gibson and Lance Parrish, as coaches. But that optimism quickly turned to despair as the Tigers lost their first nine games and were saddled with a 3–21 record by the end of April. By the All-Star break, they were sitting with a miserable 25–67 mark and had become the laughingstock of major league baseball. Before September even began, the team had already surpassed the 100-loss mark. By the time the season mercifully ended, the Tigers were 43–119, setting a new record for the most losses in AL history and coming just one loss shy of matching the 1962 New York Mets' record of 120 losses. Although three Tigers pitchers—Jeremy Bonderman, Nate Cornejo, and Mike Maroth—came close to recording 20 losses, only Maroth actually ended the season eclipsing that dismal mark. The good news was that the team rebounded to post a 72–90 record the following year and a playoff-earning 95–67 mark in 2006.

have gotten a lot of experience."

The Tigers added to that experience by bringing in such veterans as All-Star catcher Ivan Rodriguez and right fielder Magglio Ordóñez over the next two seasons. In 2006, the rebuilt Tigers were suddenly beasts, tearing to a 35–14 record to start the season, then defying the experts by leading the division up until the final game of the year. Although they lost the AL Central to the Minnesota Twins in the end, they captured the Wild Card berth into the playoffs and then made the most of it, upsetting the favored New York Yankees in the AL Division Series (ALDS) and then sweeping the Oakland Athletics in the ALCS to reach the World Series.

The Tigers couldn't quite complete the fairy-tale season, losing to the St. Louis Cardinals four games to one, but the roar had been restored in Detroit. And with such rising stars as Bonderman, AL Rookie of the Year pitcher Justin Verlander, and center fielder Curtis Granderson, the Tigers were built for the long haul. "They're a wonderful group of guys," said Jim Leyland, a veteran big-league skipper in his first year as manager of the Tigers. "We've got a lot of things going right now."

Detroit has a history of cycling around to a championship after every prolonged slump, and after a 2006 season that made everyone recall the glory days of 1984's world championship season, today's Tigers are showing their claws again. The Detroit faithful have every reason to believe that the winning streak will continue as the Tigers try to run down yet another championship for the Motor City.